Proto-ceratops

This was a dinosaur with a beak instead
of a mouth. It lived in Mongolia and
ate grasses and plants.

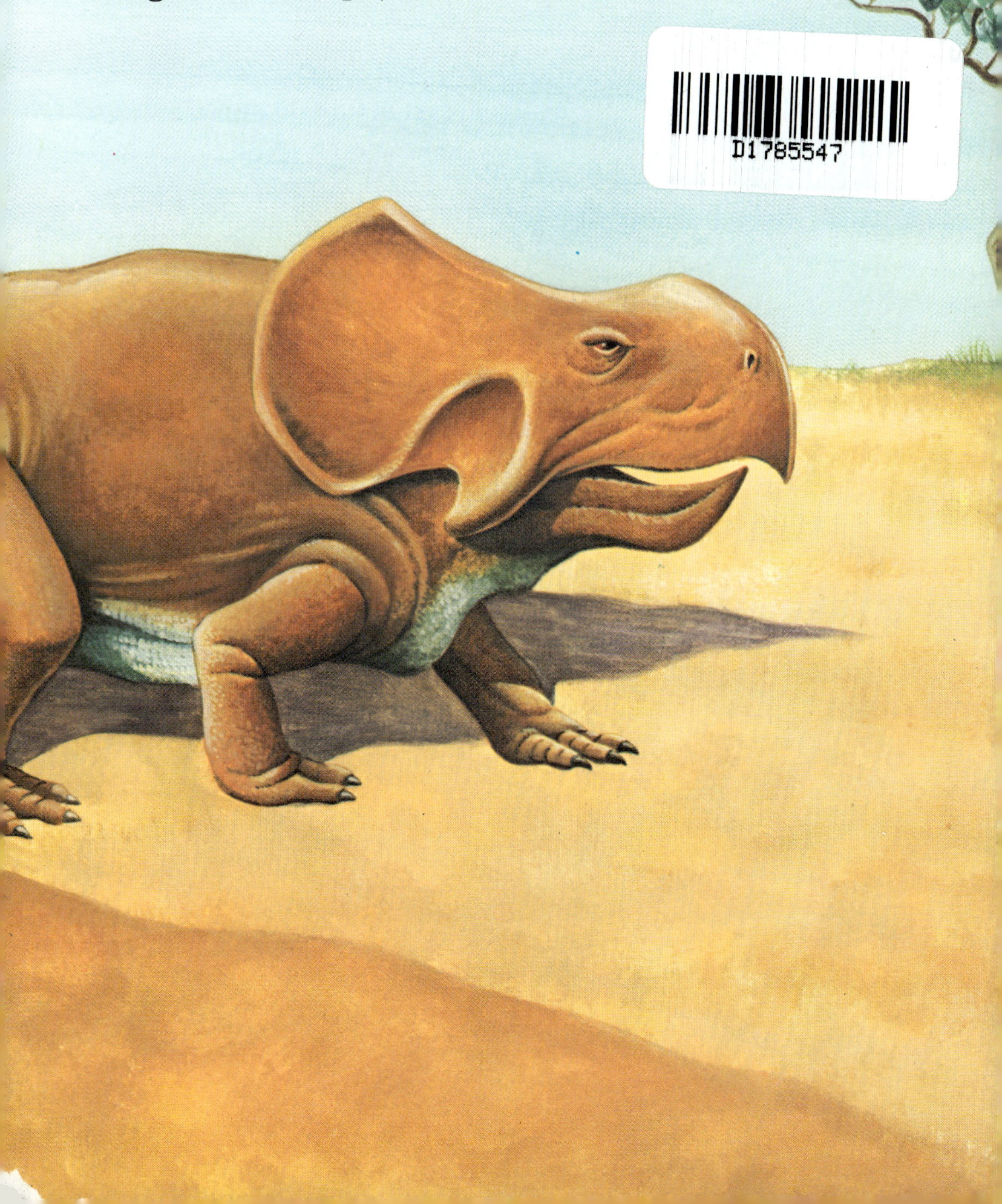

Ornitho-lestes

This was a little dinosaur which could run very fast on two legs and which ate birds by catching them with its front legs.

My First Colour Library

Prehistoric Monsters

Purnell

ISBN 0 361 03247 1
Copyright © 1975 Purnell Publishers Limited
First published 1975 by Purnell Books, Paulton,
Bristol BS18 5LQ, a member of the BPCC group
Made and printed in Great Britain by
Purnell and Sons (Book Production) Limited
Paulton, Bristol
Reprinted 1985
Written by Jane Carruth
Illustrated by Graham Allen

Diplo-docus

This dinosaur lived in North America. It ate water plants and stayed mostly in the water, as it had no sharp tusks or spikes to protect it from its enemies on land.

Ptero-dactyl

The pterodactyl was a flying reptile. It lived on the sea-shore and in the woods, and at night it hung upside down like a bat.

Tricer-atops

The triceratops was a dinosaur
with three horns on its head. It
lived about fifty million years
ago near swamps, and ate plants
and leaves from the trees.

Bronto-saurus

The brontosaurus was a huge reptile with a tiny brain. It had feet like an elephant and probably lived in lakes as well as on dry land.

Styraco-saurus

This dinosaur looked a bit like a rhinoceros and had a long spiked horn on its nose. It lived in Canada.

Stego-saurus

This was a strange dinosaur, with lots of bony spines to protect its body, but it was quite harmless and ate only grasses and plants.

Woolly Rhino-cerus

The woolly rhinocerus lived in Siberia and was a huge dangerous animal about six feet high. It ate mostly twigs and leaves, and herbs and grass in summer. It lived at the same time as early man, who hunted and ate it.

Archae-opteryx

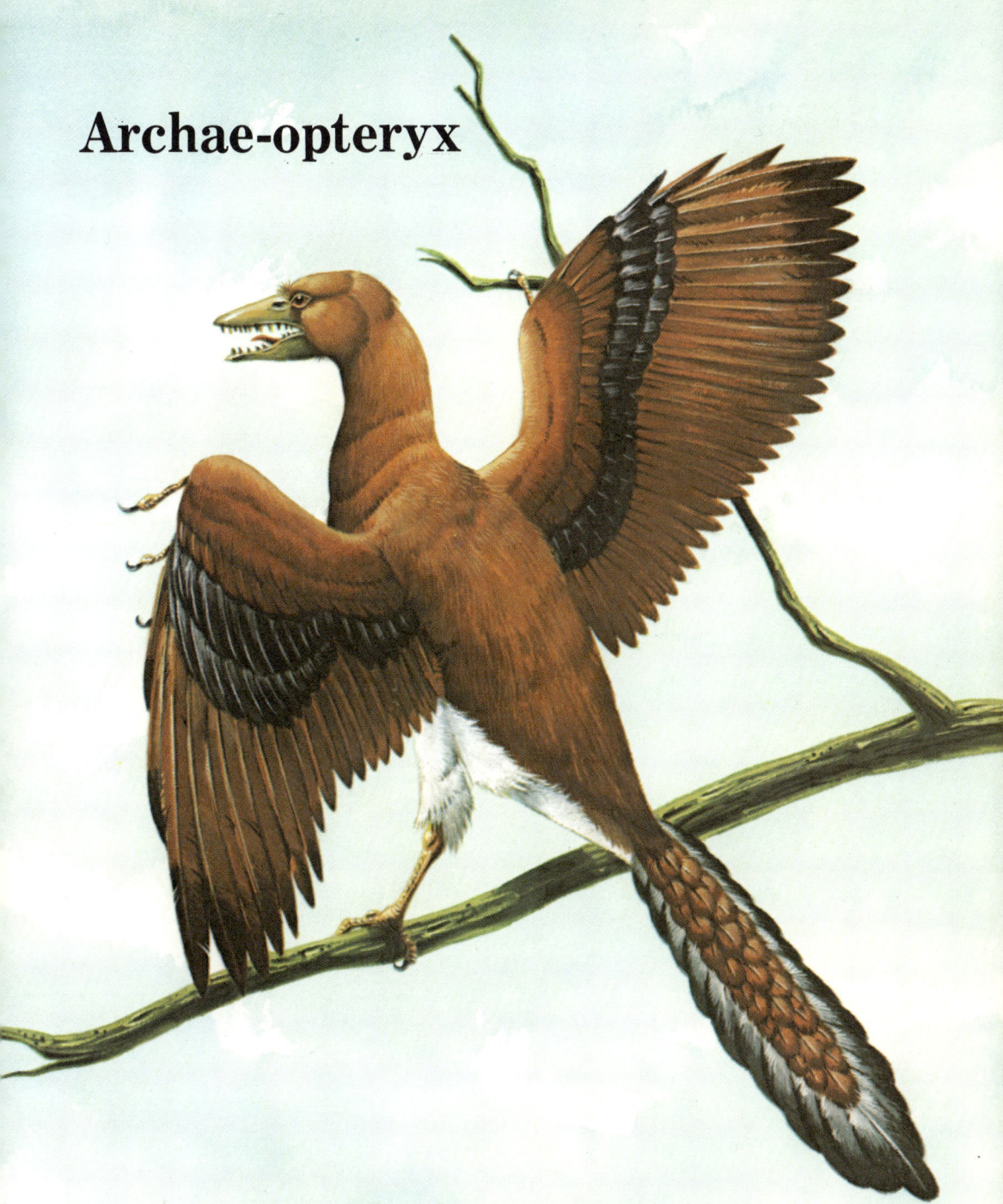

Archaeopteryx was the first bird, and was only a bit bigger than a pigeon. It was not very good at flying and ate mostly fruit and berries and small insects.

Brachio-saurus

The brachiosaurus was eighty feet long. It lived in deep water in Eastern Africa and North America, and could walk on the sea-bed with its long neck above the surface.

Plesio-saurus

This was a swimming reptile with a small head and a long neck. It used its long neck to reach out and catch small fish to eat.

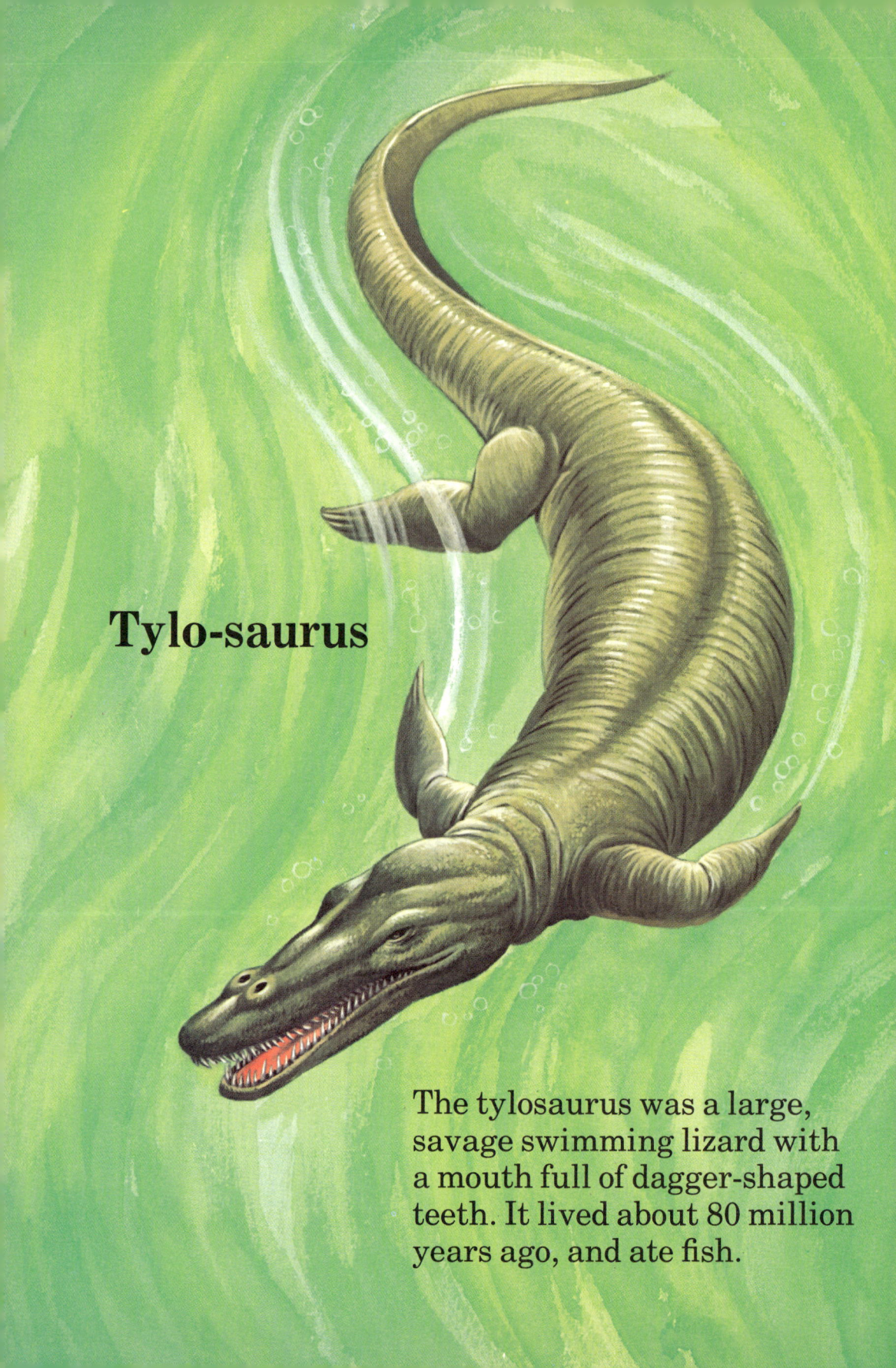

Tylo-saurus

The tylosaurus was a large, savage swimming lizard with a mouth full of dagger-shaped teeth. It lived about 80 million years ago, and ate fish.

Iguan-odon

This was a dinosaur which often stood upright and ran very fast on two legs like a man.

Tyranno-saurus

The tyrannosaurus was a giant dinosaur with a huge head and six-inch-long teeth. It was one of the largest of all meat-eating dinosaurs.

This reptile was rather like a funny looking lizard with a strange 'sail' on its back made of bone and skin.

Dimetro-don

This was a big flying reptile with wings which were twenty-seven feet wide. It ate fish and glided down to the water to catch them.

Pterano-don

Mega-therium

This was a stupid animal which ate leaves on trees.
It was as big as an elephant and lived in America.

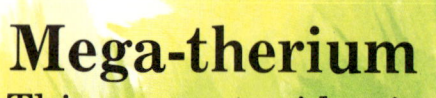

Eo-hippus

This animal was the first horse. It was about as big as a fox and ate mostly soft juicy swamp plants and leaves of bushes.

Smilo-don

This was a tiger with long sharp teeth which lived in California. It attacked and ate all kinds of animals which went down to the lakes to drink, and was even feared by elephants.

Mam-moth